TopReaders

Under the Sea

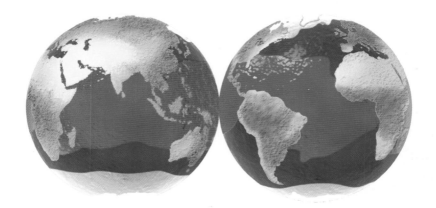

Denise Ryan

Contents

Oceans are huge areas of water that make up more than two-thirds of our planet.

The Seafloor

Hills and mountains rise from the seafloor . Deep valleys go down to the ocean depths .

mountain

Many of these hills and mountains do not reach the ocean's surface. Some poke through as islands.

valley

In the Depths

Strange creatures live on
the seafloor. There may
be more creatures living in
the depths of the ocean
than on the land or
in the air!

mussel

A **submersible** explores the ocean depths.

deep-sea "chimney"

eelpout

tube worm

orca

seal

The Food Chain

The ocean's food chain begins
with tiny creatures called
plankton . It finishes with
huge creatures such as the orca !

The plankton are eaten by small fish.
The small fish are eaten by bigger fish.
The bigger fish are eaten by seals,
and the seals are eaten by orcas.

big fish

small fish

The Water Cycle

The Sun's heat causes water from the ocean to evaporate , or turn into gas. It cools to form clouds and falls back to Earth as rain. Rivers carry some water back to the ocean.

Clouds form over the sea.

Rain falls
over the land.

Water travels
underground
to the sea.

Earth's water goes round
and round in an endless cycle.

Ocean Habitats

Oceans are rich in life. Some plants and animals live in the icy polar seas. Many more live in the warm waters of the tropical regions.

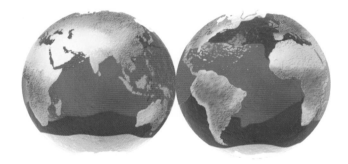

Key
- polar regions
- temperate regions
- tropical regions

The temperate regions lie between the polar seas and the tropical seas.

temperate seas

polar seas

tropical seas

Ocean Zones

Ocean waters are divided into three zones. Most sea creatures live in the top, or sunlight zone. Below that is the twilight zone, and then the dark zone, where only a few animals can survive.

dark zone

The deepest part of the ocean is far away from the shore.

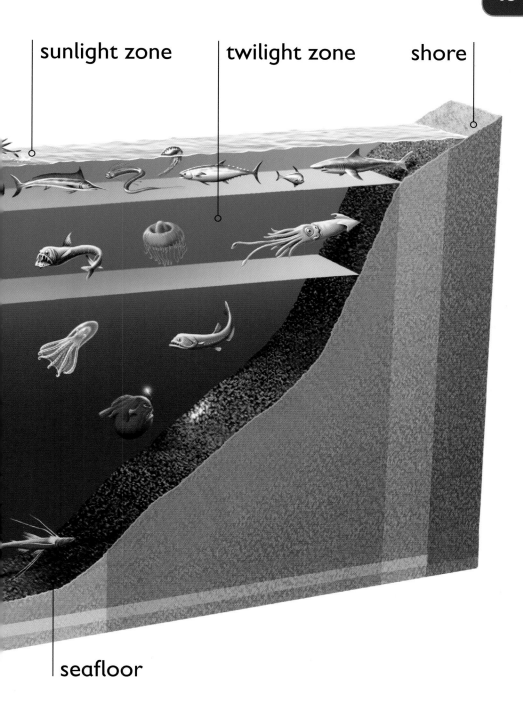

sunlight zone

twilight zone

shore

seafloor

Sometimes, divers find treasure under the sea.

discovering ancient pots on the seafloor

Underwater Treasure

Many wrecks lie on the seafloor. Divers explore them to learn about how people lived in the past.

floating a pot to the surface

Watery Clues

Underwater treasure can give us many clues about life long ago. The treasures are collected carefully, so they are not damaged.

sucking up sand

Scientists use special cameras to take photos of underwater treasure.

mapping an underwater site

Inside a Sub

The ocean floor is many miles below the surface. The only way to get there is by a small submarine called a submersible.

hatchet fish

gulper shark

Inside a submersible, scientists can study ocean plants and animals.

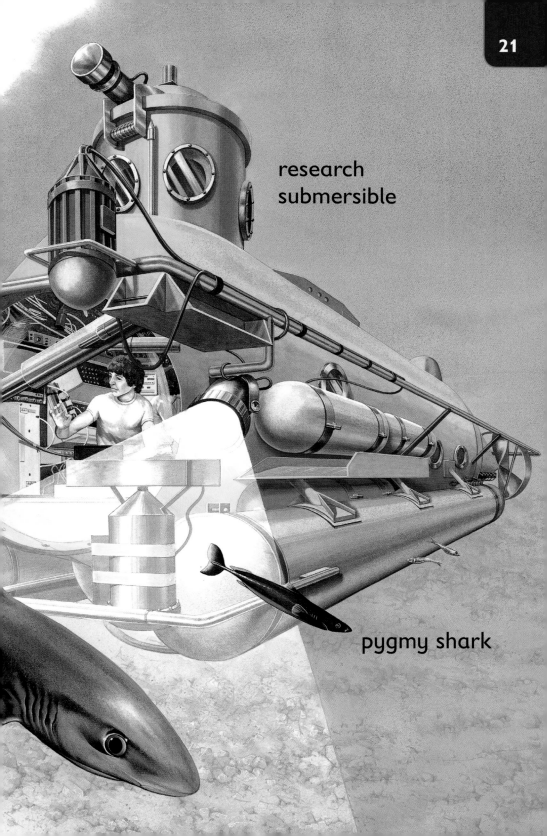

research
submersible

pygmy shark

Up Close

People who want to
see sharks go into the
ocean in shark cages.
Sharks do not attack
the cages but they do
come up close!

These great white sharks
want a closer look at
people, too!

Sea Legends

Sailors once told stories of huge sea creatures, mermaids, and strange monsters.

Sea monsters are attacking a ship. Can you see the one like a giant octopus?

Ocean Mysteries

Many years ago, empty sailing ships were found drifting in the ocean. No one knows if the crews left the ships and rowed to shore, or if they drowned.

The *Marie Celeste* was found drifting in the Atlantic Ocean in 1872. The crew had mysteriously disappeared.

The Ocean's Riches

Oil and gas are formed deep under the ocean. The machinery that drills for them is on a platform. Some platforms are attached to the seafloor. Others are like floating islands.

Oil is so valuable it is sometimes called "black gold."

Workers fly to the platforms
by helicopter. They live and work
there for weeks at a time.

helicopter

Quiz

Can you match the pictures with their names?

oil platform   diver

oceans   submersible

Glossary

depths: the part of the ocean near the seafloor

eelpout: a fish that lives near the seafloor

evaporate: to turn from liquid to gas

orca: another name for a killer whale

plankton: tiny organisms that float in ocean currents

platform: a raised surface, like a floor

polar: around the North and South poles

scientists: people trained in science

seafloor: the land at the bottom of the ocean

submersible: an underwater ship that is shaped like a small submarine

temperate: not too hot, and not too cold

tropical: around the equator

Index